SECRET STRATEGIES FOR MAKING MONEY

ETHICALLY CREATING WEALTH WITH INTEGRITY

DR. JAGADEESH PILLAI

Made with ♥ on the Notion Press Platform
www.notionpress.com

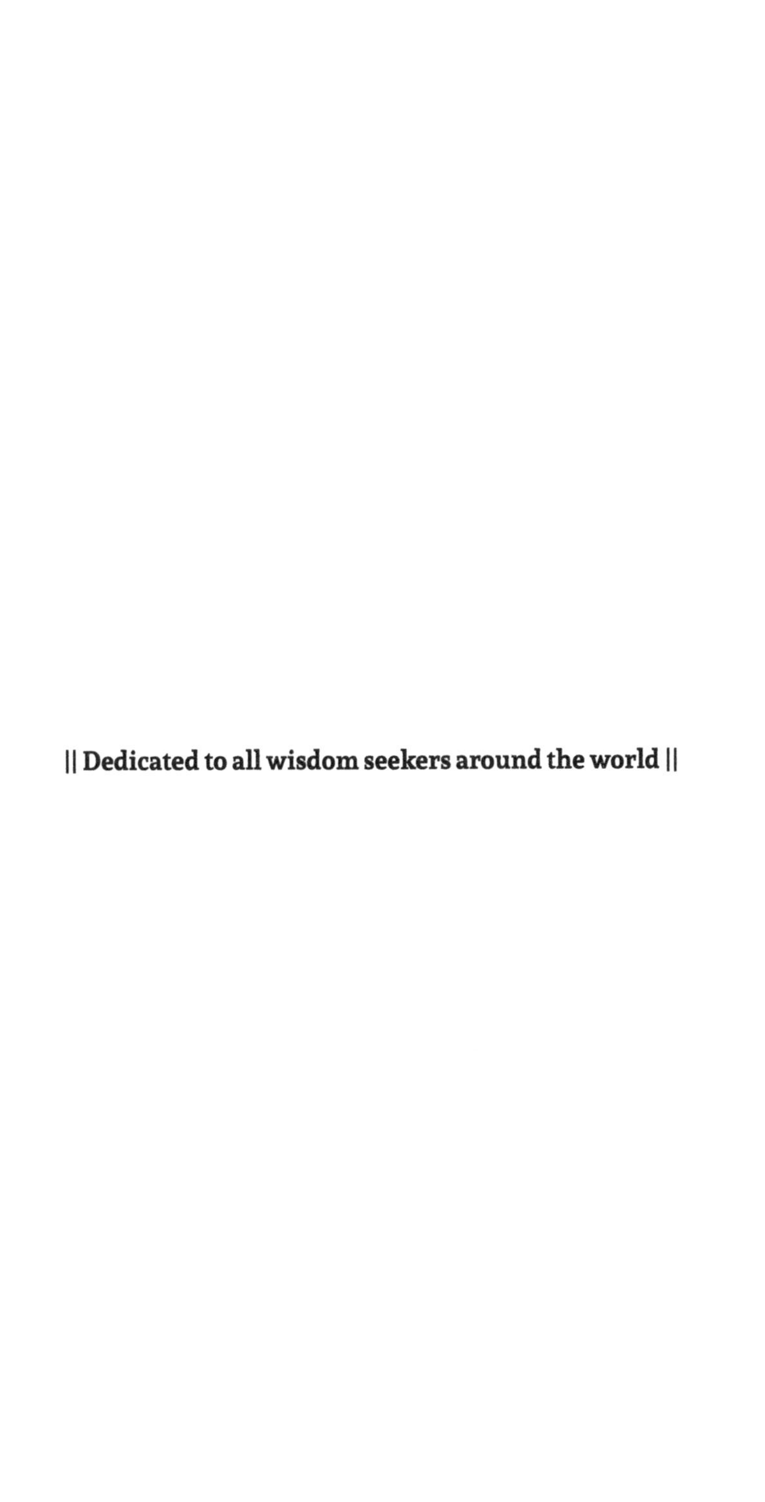

|| Dedicated to all wisdom seekers around the world ||

Contents

Contents

PRAYER

"Om Bhadram Karnebhih Shrunuyaama DevaahBhadram Pashyemaakshabhiryajatraah Sthirairangaistushtuvaamsastanoobhih Vyashema Devahitam YadaayuhSwasti Na Indro VridhashravaahSwasti Nah Pooshaa VishwavedaahSwasti Nastaarkshyo ArishtanemihSwasti No Brihaspatir DadhaatuOm Shantih, Shantih, Shantih"

The literal meaning of this mantra is: OM. O Gods! Let us hear auspicious words from our ears. O reverent Gods! Let us behold propitious visions from our eyes, let our organs and body be stable, healthy, and strong. Let us do that which is pleasing to the gods in the life span allotted to us. May Indra, inscribed in the scriptures, bring us fortune! May Pushan, the knower of the world, grant us prosperity! May Trakshya, who vanquishes enemies, bestow us with blessings! May Brihaspati bring us success!
OM Peace, Peace, Peace.

ABOUT THE AUTHOR

Dr. Jagadeesh Pillai is a renowned Guinness World Record holder, writer, and researcher hailing from Varanasi, also known as the abode of Lord Shiva. With a Ph.D. in Vedic Science and a range of creative ideas and achievements, he is a true polymath. He is the author of more than 100 books including Research Publications. Although his roots can be traced back to Kerala, the people of Varanasi hold him in high regard and affectionately consider him one of their own.

Dr. Pillai has achieved four Guinness World Records in the following subjects:

"Script to Screen" - In this record, Dr. Pillai produced and directed an animation film within the shortest time possible, breaking the previous record set by Canadians. He has also received numerous national and international awards and recognitions for this achievement.

Longest Line of Postcards - For this record, Dr. Pillai created a line of 16,300 postcards on the occasion of the 163rd anniversary of Indian Postal Day. The event also included a questionnaire about the Indian flag.

Largest Poster Awareness Campaign - Dr. Pillai designed an awareness campaign on the subject of "Beti Bachao - Beti Padhao" (Save the Girl Child - Educate the Girl Child) to achieve this record.

Largest Envelope - In tribute to the Indian Prime Minister's

"Make in India" initiative, Dr. Pillai created a 4000 square meter envelope using waste paper to achieve this record.

Attempted - **70000 Candles on a 210 kg Cake** - To celebrate the 70th Indian Independence Day, Dr. Pillai attempted to light 70,000 candles on a 210 kg cake, which was recorded in World Records India.

Attempted - **Documentary on Dhamek Stupa of Sarnath in 17 Languages** - Dr. Pillai attempted to create a documentary on the Dhamek Stupa of Sarnath, dubbing it in 17 different languages. The result of this attempt is currently awaiting confirmation from the Guinness World Records.

Dr. Pillai is skilled in teaching the Bhagavad Gita, a Hindu scripture, and is popular among young people. He has helped many young people improve their lives through his motivational teachings.

In addition to teaching, he has composed and sung numerous Sanskrit Bhajans and patriotic songs.

He has also written and directed several short films and documentaries for awareness campaigns, and has volunteered with the police in both UP and Kerala to spread awareness about various issues through videos and photography.

Incredibly, he has produced and directed over 100 documentaries about the city of Varanasi, all on his own.

He has also helped and guided more than 25 boys and girls to achieve world records through creative and innovative methods. He is a multifaceted person who uses his intellect and the blessings given to him by God to excel in various areas. He is both a teacher and a student, always learning and teaching, and is able to master any subject he comes across.

He is a selfless social activist and motivational speaker who has overcome struggles and failures to become a successful and enthusiastic individual with a rich life experience.

In addition to his work with the Bhagavad Gita, he is also an efficient Tarot card reader, Astro-Vastu consultant, and a talented singer and composer. He has sung the entire Ram Charita Manas and Bhagavad Gita in his own compositions, and has sung the phrase "Lokah Samastha Sukhino Bhavantu" in 50 different languages. He is currently working on a detailed and scientific study of Vedas, Upanishads, Puranas, and the Bhagavad Gita. He has also composed and sung the Hanuman Chalisa and Gayatri Mantra in 108 and 1008 different compositions, respectively.

Awards - Four Times Guinness World Records, Winner of Mahatma Gandhi Vishwa Shanti Puraskar, Mahatma Gandhi Global Peace Ambassador, Kashi Ratna Award, Dr. APJ Abdul Kalam Motivational Person of the Year 2017, Mother Teresa Award, Indira Gandhi Priyadarshini Award, Bharat Vikas Ratna Award, Udyog Ratna Award, Vigyan Prasar Award, Poorvanchal Ratn Samman.

PREFACE

This book, "Secret Strategies for Making Money Ethically: Creating Wealth with Integrity," provides readers with an in-depth exploration of ethical investing. Through eleven chapters, readers will gain a comprehensive understanding of the principles of ethical investing, the benefits of sustainable investing, the role of corporate governance, the impact of ESG investing, the benefits of socially responsible investing, the principles of impact investing, the role of social impact investing, the role of investor advocacy, the benefits of philanthropic investing, and the impact of ethical investing on society.

This book is an invaluable resource for anyone looking to make money ethically and create wealth with integrity. It provides readers with the knowledge and tools to make informed decisions about their investments and to understand the implications of their choices. With this book, readers will gain a better understanding of the power of ethical investing and the positive impact it can have on society.

I

Introduction to Ethical Investing

Ethical investing is gaining popularity among investors looking to make money both sustainably and ethically. This type of investing, also known as socially responsible investing, involves investing in assets that have either a positive ethical or environmental impact, support social welfare, or are otherwise deemed ethical. By investing responsibly, investors can contribute to advancing society and respect the environment, while still making money through their investments.

Benefits of Ethical Investing

One of the key benefits of ethical investing is that it allows investors to make informed decisions about both their investments and the companies involved. Investors know exactly how their money is being used, and can choose companies with a good track record in ethical behaviour.

As such, it can be immensely satisfying to see your investments making a positive ethical and environmental impact.

In addition, there are often tax incentives to ethical investing. Many investments in ethical companies receive favourable tax treatment, and can provide significant economic benefits to investors.

Risks of Ethical Investing

As with any investment, ethical investing comes with some risks. The most important is the risk of financially committing to companies that do not necessarily share the same values and beliefs as the investor. This could lead to losses if the company is not doing well, or if it is not adhering to ethical standards.

Another risk of ethical investing is the lack of liquidity. Although many of these investments can generate reasonable returns, they may not be as liquid as other investments, meaning investors could be unable to access their money in an efficient manner. Furthermore, because these investments often take longer to mature, there is also an opportunity cost when time is not taken into account.

Finding Ethical Investments

The best way to find ethical investments is to work with an individual advisor or a financial institution. An advisor can provide guidance and help navigate any possible pitfalls. Financial institutions can also provide access to ethical investments to their clients. Additionally, investors can source investments from socially responsible financial firms that specialize in specific areas thus giving them access to detailed research and market insights.

Conclusion

In conclusion, ethical investing is a sound way to make money and contribute to positive societal change. However, it is important to be aware of the risks associated with these investments and be sure to do the necessary research before committing any money. With the right financial advisor and careful consideration, ethical investing can be an incredibly rewarding and profitable activity.

"Wealth is not the same as money. Wealth is in the form of ideas, knowledge, and creativity that can generate income."

- Robert Kiyosaki

II

2. Understanding the Principles of Ethical Investing

In today's globalized and increasingly interconnected society, the principles of ethical money making are more important than ever. In order to be successful in the modern business world, it is essential to understand the underlying principles of ethical money making. By doing this, one can ensure that their financial success is built on a strong and sustainable foundation of ethical creativity, responsibility, and respect.

Firstly, one must be creative in their approach to making money. Instead of relying solely on traditional sources of income, one must always strive to seek new and innovative opportunities to generate wealth. This could involve exploring new industries, products, services and technologies with potential to generate significant returns.

By keeping an open mind and seeking out new business opportunities, one can develop innovative solutions to earn money in an ethical and responsible fashion.

Secondly, it is essential to be responsible when approaching money making. Rather than promised quick-fix solutions, lasting wealth comes from thoughtful, responsible actions. This means building a reputation and relationship with others through consistency, fairness and honesty in business transactions. It is also essential to consider the ethical implications of each financial decision and prioritize long-term stability over short-term gains.

Finally, respect for others is paramount in ethical money making. People are the cornerstone of any successful business endeavor and it is essential to recognize and embrace the diverse talents and perspectives that each team member brings to the table. This means taking the time to be attentive to team members' ideas and creating an environment of mutual respect and collaboration. Furthermore, organizations should prioritize ethics and sustainability throughout all aspects of their operations, from manufacturing practices to customer service.

Understanding the principles of ethical money making is essential to success in today's globalized business environment. By being creative, responsible and respectful when approaching money making activities, one can build a strong and sustainable foundation for success and ensure that their financial success is ethically and responsibly generated.

Exploring the principles of ethical investing is essential for anyone looking to make money in a responsible and sustainable way. By taking a creative, responsible, and respectful approach to money making, one can ensure that their financial success is built on a strong and ethical foundation.

Creativity is key when it comes to making money ethically. Instead of relying solely on traditional sources of income, one must always strive to seek out new and innovative opportunities to generate wealth. This could involve exploring new industries, products, services, and technologies with potential to generate significant returns.

Responsibility is also essential when it comes to ethical money making. Rather than promised quick-fix solutions, lasting wealth comes from thoughtful, responsible actions. This means building a reputation and relationship with others through consistency, fairness, and honesty in business transactions. It is also important to consider the ethical implications of each financial decision and prioritize long-term stability over short-term gains.

Finally, respect for others is paramount in ethical money making. People are the cornerstone of any successful business endeavor and it is essential to recognize and embrace the diverse talents and perspectives that each team member brings to the table. This means taking the time to be attentive to team members' ideas and creating an environment of mutual respect and collaboration. By taking these steps, one can ensure that their financial success is built on a strong and ethical foundation.

"Making money is easy. It's. It's spending less than you make and investing the rest wisely."

- Dave Ramsey

ജ

III

Exploring the Benefits of Sustainable Investing

Sustainable investing places an emphasis on investments that promote a socially conscious and environmentally conscious approach to wealth management. Sustainable investing actively and intentionally seeks to minimize "negative externalities", and instead promote a positive management of money in order to maximize positive impact for both the environment and people. In examining the benefits of sustainable investing, one must consider the positive financial, societal, and environmental impacts.

In terms of financial benefits, sustainable investing can lead to an improved public perception of a business, which can lead to increased investor confidence and potential revenues. Companies that exercise sustainable investing often benefit from increased sales, better access to capital, reduced risk of disruptive regulation, and improved access to new customers. Additionally, sustainable investing can provide a number of tax benefits, such as tax credits and exemptions.

In terms of societal benefits, sustainable investing can lead to the improvement of livelihoods and lives. It can be a tool for generating positive social change, supporting businesses, and creating a more equitable and fair matrix for investing. As an example, many forms of ethical investing support those who are not traditionally included in the investor pool, by giving equal weight to all potential investments, regardless of the background or status of the business. Sustainable investing can also increase the amount of resources available to charitable organizations, while offering smaller, targeted philanthropic opportunities to individuals and businesses.

Finally, in terms of environmental benefits, sustainable investing can minimize the environmental footprint of investing activities. Sustainable investments can limit exposure to fossil fuels, promote clean energy sources, and invest in projects with low environmental impact. By investing in industries such as renewable energy and other green technologies it can be possible to reduce emissions, clean up the environment, and slow down climate change.

In short, sustainable investing presents the potential for financial, societal, and environmental benefits. From improving access to capital and creating a more equitable investor landscape, to improving the sustainability of the environment and having a positive impact on human and animal life, sustainable investing offers a wide range of advantages. Any investor who is interested in improving the benefits of their investing decisions should certainly consider the potential of sustainable investing for positive financial and societal returns.

"The most important thing is integrity. If you can fake that, you've got it made."

- George Burns

ƐƆ

IV

Understanding the Role of Corporate Governance

The term corporate governance ethical money making is a broad one. It encompasses aspects of corporate management and the responsibilities of organizational leadership when it comes to using the collected resources and capital to pursue ethical and responsible goals. The purpose of this essay is to provide a comprehensive understanding of what corporate governance ethical money making is and its important implications for modern business organizations.

At its core, corporate governance ethical money making is the process of integrating ethical principles into the decision-making processes of corporate entities. It is an attempt to create regulations that ensure that businesses respect the expectations of society when it comes to ethical issues like transparency and accountability. It involves understanding a company's ethical and legal responsibilities and developing policies and procedures to ensure these responsibilities are met.

This can include having an appropriate board of directors to review important decisions, implementing systems of checks and balances, following a code of ethical conduct, ensuring compliance with applicable laws and regulations, and using financial and accounting systems that promote transparency and accountability. Companies must also closely monitor their policies and procedures in order to ensure they continue to be followed in a responsible manner.

At the same time, corporate governance ethical money making is also about making sure that decisions are made in an ethical and responsible manner to promote long-term success. Companies must strive to create a culture of honesty and integrity in which the interests of all stakeholders, including shareholders, executives, employees, and the community, are taken into consideration. This includes considering the long-term effects of decisions, and investing money in ways that promote a company's organizational goals, contribute to the community it operates in and create a positive impact on the environment.

In short, corporate governance ethical money making requires businesses to evaluate the ethical, legal and social implications of decisions related to the use of funds and resources. It is a complex process that requires organizations to create appropriate governance structures, understand the ethical responsibilities of business management, and implement systems that promote transparency, accountability and responsibility. Only with a comprehensive approach to this important issue can businesses ensure that their decisions are in alignment with the expectations of society and promote a meaningful contribution to the community in which they operate.

"Money is a terrible master but an excellent servant."

- P.T. Barnum

ꙮ

V

Examining the Impact of ESG Investing

The concept of ethical investing, otherwise known as ESG (Environmental, Social, and Governance) investing, has risen to prominence over recent years. With its origins dating back to 1971, ESG investing seeks to create long-term wealth while also considering the environmental, social, and governance (ESG) aspects of a given company's operations. In this essay, an examination of the impact of ESG investing will occur, taking into account its current trend, potential benefits, and potential risks.

Firstly, it must be stated that ESG investing has become increasingly popular. In 2018, $6.57 trillion was invested using ethical criteria, which accounts for more than 15% of all dollars invested globally. This trend has been encouraged by a heightened level of awareness among investors regarding the potential benefits that ethical investments can bring, but also by a range of ESG scoring products developed by companies such as MSCI and S&P, which enable investors to easily monitor the ESG profile of different investments.

The potential impacts of ESG investing are varied and potentially powerful. Firstly, ESG investing encourages the development of long-term wealth, as it encourages the reduction of energy expenses associated with the production of a given product. This reduction in energy expenses can extend to the long-term health of a business, as well as that of the environment. Additionally, as ESG investing focuses on encouraging transparency and good governance practices, companies that comply with ESG investment principles may be better managed and less likely to experience financial distress in the long-term.

Despite its potential benefits, there are potential risks associated with ESG investing. Firstly, the extent to which specific companies comply with ESG principles can be difficult to judge and may be open to a range of subjective interpretations. Secondly, it should be noted that ethical investing can be linked to a range of legal and regulatory issues, which can be difficult for investors to navigate. Thus, investors must be sure to abide by applicable rules when incorporating ESG principles into their investment strategies.

To conclude, although ESG investing has been subject to increased attention over recent years, it is important for investors to understand its potential benefits and risks. From encouraging long-term wealth development and greater governance practices to increasing the risk of legal or regulatory issues, ESG investing should be carefully considered before being implemented.

"The only way to do great work is to love what you do. If you haven't found it yet, keep looking. Don't settle. As with all matters of the heart, you'll know when you find it."

- Steve Jobs

ꕤ

VI

Analyzing the Benefits of Socially Responsible Investing

Socially responsible investing (SRI) is an approach to investing that takes into account environmental, social, and corporate governance (ESG) criteria with the goal of generating long-term, sustainable returns. The approach is gaining in popularity, especially among the younger generations of investors. While the performance of an SRI portfolio may not always outperform traditional investing, there are several advantages to this approach that all investors should consider.

First, when an investor selects a company for an SRI portfolio, they are able to research the company's practices to ensure that they are in alignment with their own values and social beliefs. For example, an investor may be interested in avoiding companies that engage in animal testing. Conducting due diligence on a company to ensure that no animal testing is part of its operations is an important factor to consider when constructing a portfolio of SRI stocks.

Next, there are environmental benefits to SRI investing. Many of the companies in an SRI portfolio are working to reduce their carbon footprint through green initiatives such as offsetting their emissions or investing in renewable sources of energy. These companies are also often aligned with the Paris Agreement's goals of keeping global warming below two degrees Celsius above pre-industrial levels, and investing in these companies can be a way to express solidarity with these global objectives.

SRI also has a reputation for engaging more with the companies it invests in. Many SRI investors are interested in becoming more actively involved with the companies they are investing in, and they may engage with company management to advocate for changes in policies or operations to reflect their values or to further improve the company's impact on the world. This can be a way to ensure that a company's operations and policies continuously improve while taking into account the investor's personal values or beliefs.

Finally, due to its increasing popularity, SRI investing is quickly becoming part of the mainstream. As this trend gains greater acceptance, it is increasingly likely that companies will begin to adopt SRI practices in an effort to secure investment from the growing number of investors dedicated to this approach.

Socially responsible investing can be a great way for investors to express solidarity with environmental, ethical and social values, while also mitigating risk. Although the performance of an SRI portfolio may not always outperform a traditional portfolio, there are many benefits to this approach, making it a great choice for many investors.

"It's not about how much money you make, but about how much money you keep, how hard it works for you, and how many generations you keep it for."

- Robert Kiyosaki

ꕥ

VII

Understanding the Principles of Impact Investing

Impact investing is an investing strategy that seeks to generate both financial and social outcomes. It typically involves investing capital into projects that are projected to generate positive social, environmental, or economic impacts while also providing investors the opportunity to earn an expected return on their investment. While it is often misunderstood, the principles of impact investing can be clearly defined.

The primary objective of impact investing is to yield measurable impacts and return on capital. As a result, investors seek to identify investments that will create social or environmental benefits in addition to earning financial returns. They focus on achieving positive, pre-defined outcomes through their investments and use market-based solutions to achieve social or environmental goals.

The considerations of impact investing are broader than just the financial return. In addition to financial projections, impact investors must also consider a wide range of qualitative and quantitative elements when evaluating potential investments. They must consider factors such as the potential for impact, the scalability of the investment, the sustainability of the impact over the long-term, and the impact's public perception.

In addition to these factors, impact investors also need to be mindful of the risks associated with their investments. While there is an expectation of financial return, impact investors are also exposed to potential regulatory or reputational risks as a result of their investments. As a result, investors should ensure that their investments comply with relevant laws, regulations, and standards in order to minimize their exposure to risk.

Ultimately, impact investing is a complex and specialized field that requires careful consideration and expertise. As a result, impact investors should understand the principles of impact investing, consult experienced advisors, and carefully consider both the positive and negative impacts of their investments before making a commitment. By doing so, investors can ensure that their investments will lead to both financial and social returns and create meaningful, long-term impacts.

"The more money you make, the more money you can give away."

- Oprah Winfrey

℘

VIII

Examining the Role of Social Impact Investing

Social Impact Investing, also known as Impact Investing or Impact Finance, refers to an investment that is specifically focused on achieving a social or environmental purpose. This could refer to anything from providing educational opportunities for disadvantaged communities to clean energy projects that reduce greenhouse gas emissions. The goal of social impact investing is to drive social and environmental change while also generating a financial return.

Social Impact Investing is comprised of a variety of forms of investments, including direct investments and venture capital. Direct investments involve a direct and direct ownership of an impact-oriented asset such as a microfinance loan, while venture capital investments involve the private financing of social enterprises. Impact investments can be made through private, public, and nonprofit institutions or through private individuals.

The Role of Social Impact Investing is to facilitate investments that both contribute to a better future and generate returns. This is accomplished through a focus on both sides of the balance sheet – financial returns and social/environmental impact. Social Impact Investing provides capital to ventures and/or organizations that are focused on creating positive social and/or environmental change in order to generate returns of capital for investors.

The success of Social Impact Investing is contingent upon many factors, including the selection of a qualified investment manager, the identification of social and environmental impact objectives, the selection of suitable investments, the monitoring and assessment of performance, the measurement of impact, the development and implementation of plans to achieve impact objectives, and the reporting of impact results.

To ensure the success of Social Impact Investing, there should be strong collaboration between investors, social entrepreneurs and philanthropists, and policy makers. This collaboration encourages the creation and implementation of new strategies and business models that can benefit society and provide investment opportunities.

Social Impact Investing has the potential to contribute to a better future by helping to address some of the world's pressing social and environmental challenges. By taking both financial returns and social/environmental returns into consideration, investors can help to drive these goals while still generating attractive returns. By engaging the wider social sector in its work, Social Impact Investing can further contribute to the creation and implementation of effective strategies and business models that can benefit society and yield returns for investors.

"The way to wealth depends on just two words, industry and frugality; that is, waste neither time nor money, but make the best use of both."

- Benjamin Franklin

ꕤ

IX

Understanding the Role of Investor Advocacy

Investor advocacy is a form of activism in which shareholders use their collective power to influence corporate activities. It is a growing trend as investors increasingly take an active role in corporate governance and seek to use their financial power to ensure that companies not only grow but also remain accountable to the people they serve.

The most common form of investor advocacy is when shareholders use the power of their ownership to influence corporate actions and attitudes. Shareholders can leverage their ownership of company stock by voting their shares to reject executive compensation plans, oppose mergers and acquisition, and speak out against environmental or labor practices. Through the filing of shareholder resolutions and the use of proxy voting, shareholders can call upon senior management to take action on matters that may be detrimental to the success of the company. At its most effective, investor advocacy allows investors to ensure that the companies they own remain ethical and financially sound.

The second major form of investor advocacy is when investors use their financial power to invest in companies that practice responsible and ethical behavior. By investing in companies with positive environmental records, good corporate governance, and sustainable practices, investors can send a powerful message to corporate officers and board members that they will be held accountable when they act irresponsibly.

Finally, investor advocacy can encompass promoting socially responsible investing, which involves applying a socially oriented criterion to investing decisions. This type of investing generally aims to generate both financial return and social or environmental good. It includes values-based investing, ethical investing, and impact investing.

The effectiveness of investor advocacy largely depends upon the motivations of individual shareholders. It can be used to promote powerful change in the way companies operate and affect the lives of their employees and customers, or it can be used to satisfy individual or group values and sentiments.

Whether investors are motivated to promote ethical and responsible practices or for other reasons, there is no denying that investor advocacy is an important force for progress and change in the world today. By mobilizing shareholders and utilizing their financial resources, they can ensure that companies remain socially responsible and act in the best interests of the people they serve. In this way, investor advocacy will continue to have a positive impact on the global economy and society.

"The reason most people never reach their goals is that they don't define them, or ever seriously consider them as believable or achievable. Winners can tell you where they are going, what they plan to do along the way, and who will be sharing the adventure with them."

- Denis Waitley

ꟹ

X

Exploring the Benefits of Philanthropic Investing

Philanthropic investing refers to the use of investments to support a charity, mission, concept, or public good. Rather than simply donating money, philanthropic investing seeks to use financial instruments to generate returns as well as provide necessary funding to worthwhile causes. Philanthropic investing is growing in popularity as it is both ethically principled and financially rewarding.

First and foremost, philanthropic investing, or Impact Investing, allows individuals to promote the causes and social enterprises they believe in. By purchasing the stocks, bonds, and other securities associated with a particular charity, theme, or mission, individuals are able to support the cause they care about while also obtaining a financial return. Investment returns can come directly from these specified securities as well as from impact investing funds that provide exposure to multiple causes and organizations. Impact investing also provides an opportunity for long-term donors to establish a legacy of giving by contributing to causes that have long-term social or environmental impacts.

In addition to its ethical principles, philanthropic investing can also be financially rewarding. Impact investing funds seek to generate returns similar to traditional investments while also generating a positive social or environmental impact. Investing in these funds allows individuals to obtain a financial return while, at the same time, being able to support their causes. The additional returns provided by impact investing funds can also provide a form of protection from the inherent market volatility of traditional investments.

Beyond its financial rewards and ethical principles, philanthropic investing also provides an opportunity for individuals to engage with their investments in a meaningful and rewarding way. On an individual basis, philanthropic investing often allows for a deeper level of engagement and understanding with their investments. By actively monitoring their investments and taking part in social initiatives, investors gain a more holistic understanding of the cause or organization they have invested in and ultimately become more engaged with the impact of their investments.

Philanthropic investing provides individuals with a unique

way to both support the causes they care about and reap the financial rewards that come with investing. By employing responsible investing practices and actively engaging with their investments, individuals are able to make a meaningful contribution while also seeing a much appreciated financial return. Not only is impact investing an ethical and financially rewarding option, but it is also an opportunity to become more deeply engaged with their investments and the causes they care about.

"Honesty is the best policy. If I lose mine honor, I lose myself."

- William Shakespeare

൱

XI

Examining the Impact of Ethical Investing on Society

In an age of increased environmental and social awareness, ethical investing on societal impacts has become increasingly important to investors. Ethical investing is broadly defined as investment strategies that seek to incorporate environmental, social, and governance (ESG) considerations into the decision-making process. By considering not only the financial returns of an investment, but also its environmental, economic and societal consequence, ethical investors are able to make decisions that are not only financially prudent but also socially responsible.

The implications of ethical investing on society are far-reaching and varied. Some investors seek to use their funds to promote certain social causes; this form of impact investing has become especially prominent in recent years, with many investors looking to have a direct positive effect on causes they care about. Impact investments are an important way of financing social entrepreneurs, empowering local communities, and alleviating poverty. Additionally, these investments can promote green initiatives, such as investing in green technology or promoting renewable energy sources.

Ethical investing has also had a positive effect on corporate governance and corporate sustainability. Through ESG-sensitive investing strategies, investors are encouraging companies to prioritize social and environmental responsibility and ethical practices. Consequently, companies are more likely to practice responsible corporate governance and pay greater attention to their environmental footprints. Furthermore, ethical investments can create incentives for companies to be more transparent about their operations and to engage with stakeholders in meaningful ways.

Finally, ethical investing can also spur economic growth. By investing in employee development, environmental sustainability, and other areas that promote economic growth, ethical investors are contributing to a stronger and healthier society. Furthermore, ethical investments can attract new investors and inspire others to adopt socially responsible investing practices.

Ethical investing is an important tool for promoting social and environmental responsibility, both in terms of individual investors and companies. By promoting corporate governance, sustainability and economic growth, ethical investing contributes to a more equitable and prosperous society. As awareness of ESG considerations continues to grow, ethical investing is likely to continue to be an important driver of social change.

Other Books Of The Author

1. The Moments When I Met God
2. Kashiyile Theertha Pathangal
3. GURU GYAN VANI
4. Abhiprerak Gita
5. ASSI SE JAIN GHAT TAK
6. Hopelessness of Arjuna
7. The Soul and It's True Nature
8. Sense of Action (Karma)
9. Action through Wisdom
10. Action through Wisdom
11. THEORY AND PRACTICAL OF EVERY ACTION
12. LOGICAL UNDERSTANDING OF THE SUPREME
13. THE IMPERISHABLE SUPREME
14. Yatra Nishadraj se Hanuman Ghat Tak
15. Yatra Karnatak Ghat se Raja Ghat Tak
16. Yatra Pandey Ghat se Prayagraj Ghat Tak
17. Yatra Ranjendra Prasad Ghat se Dattatreya Ghat Tak
18. YaatraSindhiya Ghat se Gwaliar Ghat Tak
19. Yatra Mangala Gauri Ghat se Hanuman Gadhi Ghat Tak
20. Yatra Gaay Ghat Se Nishad Ghat Tak
21. MAA GANGA, GHATEN EVM UTSAV
22. Ganga Arti Dev Deepavali evam Any Utsav
23. Potentials of Digitalized India
24. VEDIC CONSCIOUSNESS
25. A Brief Introduction to Vedic Science
26. Kashi ke Barah Jyotirling
27. IMPACT OF MOTIVATION
28. Let's have a Milky Way Journey
29. Color Therapy in a Nutshell

30. Rigveda in a Nutshell
31. Yajurveda in a Nutshell
32. Samveda in a Nutshell
33. Atharva Veda in a Nutshell
34. Ayushman Bhava - Ayurveda
35. Srimad Bhagavad Gita and Upanishad Connection
36. Srimad Bhagavad Gita - an attempt to summarize each chapter.
37. Facts and Impact of Nakshatra
38. Astro Gems - NAVARATNA
39. Ekadashi - A Concise Overview
40. A Concise View of Hanuman Chalisa
41. Inspirational Gita
42. Nakshatraranyam
43. Summary of 18 Mahapuranas
44. Synopsis of 18 Upa Puranas
45. Rigvediya Upanishads
46. Shukla Yajurvediya Upanishads
47. Krishna Yajurvediya Upanishads
48. Samavediya Upanishads
49. Atharvavediya Upanishads
50. The Seven Great Sages
51. From Rocket Scientist to President Dr. APJ Abdul Kalam
52. The Visionary's Voice - Quotes of Dr. APJ Abdul Kalam
53. The Wisdom of Swami Vivekananda: Insights and Inspiration from a Legendary Spiritual Teacher
54. Ayurvedic Remedies from the Garden
55. Sages and Seers
56. Rising Strong – Motivational Stories of Women
57. Beyond Flames -Mystery stories of Funeral Ghat Manikarnika
58. The Origins of Tulsi: A Look at the Mythological Roots of the Plant"

59. The Holistic Cow: A Look at the Physical, Spiritual, and Cultural Importance of Cows in India
60. Arts of Healing
61. Exploring the Divine
62. Understanding Five Elements
63. The Etymology of Ram
64. Symbols of India
65. Voice of Change (About Speeches of Great Men)
66. She Speaks (About Speeches of Great Women)
67. Patriotism on Celluloid – Brief About Patriotic Films
68. The Music of Motivation: A Brief Guide to Inspirational Film Songs
69. Unlocking the Secrets of the Dashopanishads
70. A Cultural Mosaic
71. Ancient Traditions, Modern Minds
72. Ecos of Ancient Wisdom
73. Beneath the Surface
74. From Temples to Ashrams
75. Sages of the Subcontinent
76. The Art of Healling (Ayurveda, Yoga & Naturopathy)
77. Indian Kitchen
78. The Festivals of India
79. The Indian Epics Retold
80. The Power of Mantras
81. The Indian River Ganges
82. The Indian Architecture
83. Rites of Passage
84. The Indian Silk Road
85. The Indian Literature
86. The Indian Villages
87. The Indian Folks & Crafts
88. The Way of Buddha
89. The Ramayan of Tulsidas

90. Astrological Remedies
91. The Secret Power of Motivation
92. Secret of Developing your Inner Strength
93. The Secret Path to Motivation
94. The Art and Secret of Positive Thinking
95. The Secrets of Practicing Ethical Living
96. Indian Art and Painting
97. The Indian Herbalism
98. Bharatanatyam to Kathak
99. Exploring India's Astrological Remedies
100. The Indian Festival of Flowers
101. Indian Handicrafts
102. The Splashes of Joy – India's Colour Festival

Contact

DR. JAGADEESH PILLAI

PhD in Vedic Science

Four Times Guinness World Record Holder

Winner of Mahatma Gandhi Vishwa Shanti Puraskar and Global Peace Ambassador

Gemology, Astro & Vastu Consultant - Spiritual Counselor

Consultant for designing World Record Ideas

Efficient Tarot Card Reader

9839093003

myrichindia@gmail.com

drjagadeeshpillai@facebook

drjagadeeshpillai@instagram

jagadeeshpillai@youtube

www. JAGADEESHPILLAI.com

|| LOKAHA SAMASTHAHA SUKHINO BHAVANTU ||

Printed by Libri Plureos GmbH in Hamburg,
Germany